# KELLIE'S BOOK

THE ART OF THE POSSIBLE

by

*Kellie Greenwald*

*Rayve Productions*
WINDSOR, CALIFORNIA

Rayve Productions Inc.
Box 726 Windsor CA 95492

Book Design: Heidi Would
Cover Art: Kellie Greenwald

Quantity discounts and bulk purchases of this and other books are available through Rayve Productions Inc. A portion of book sale proceeds for *Kellie's Book* will be donated to The Victory Center for Arts and Communications, a day program of The Cedars of Marin in San Anselmo, California. For more information and to place orders call toll-free 1-800-852-4890; fax 707-838-2220; or contact us online at rayvepro@aol.com or www.rayveproductions.com.

Publisher's Cataloging-in-Publication Data
Greenwald, Kellie.
Kellie's book : the art of the possible / by Kellie Greenwald.
   p.  cm.
ISBN-13: 978-1-877810-42-8 (alk.paper)
Summary: Illustrated autobiography and joyful guide for developmentally challenged people, their families, friends, providers, and educators.
1. Down syndrome 2. Baseball 3. Hank Greenwald 4. Developmental disabilities II. Title
Library of Congress Control Number: 2007932297
BISAC Subject Headings: BIO000000, FAM012000, HEA018000, JNF007000

## Acknowledgments

Doing a book is very difficult. I want to thank the people who helped me.

Susan Vickery is my teacher at the Victory Center and she taught me a lot about drawing faces and using color. She made suggestions about what to include in my book and worked very hard with me.

I want to thank Judy Kohn for designing the mockup of this book. It was the one we took to Barbara and Norm Ray, who are the publishers.

Lisa Scandurra is the Director of the Victory Center. She was also my boss when I was a part-time receptionist as well as a client. Lisa always encourages me to do my best and tells me when I don't.

*Foreword*

*This book is a celebration of life* — a reflection on life's joys from the perspective of a young woman with Down syndrome. Through Kellie Greenwald's colorful drawings and commentary, we learn that what makes Kellie's days beautiful and fulfilling shares so much in common with what makes our own lives beautiful and fulfilling. The message Kellie conveys on these pages may at first glance appear simple, but it is deeply profound. Kellie gives an important voice to people with disabilities, voices we have too often silenced. Kellie's reflections on the wonders of her life are telling us that "I am a person just like you." If we take but a moment to look at life's beauty through the eyes of this inviting, talented 29 year old, we will see beauty, too.

*Kellie's Book* is a source of hope for families of children with disabilities. It is a testament to the fact that when children know they are utterly loved and supported, there is no end to what they can achieve and no end to what they give back by uplifting the lives of those around them. Far more important than the three R's in getting along in life is believing in oneself and nurturing a personality and social skills that grace every moment. Kellie's drawings, full of life and charm, so poignantly exemplify this message. In this book Kellie teaches us to view her as a person first, and not to judge her by her disability, and that differences among people are, after all, what make life so interesting and make the world go around.

Kellie, thank you for teaching us this important lesson.

Corinne R. Smith, Ph.D.
Professor and former Dean of Education
Syracuse University
Coauthor, *Learning Disabilities: A to Z*

## A Note from Teacher Susan Vickery

Enthusiasm, tenacity, and sincerity flood each moment of Kellie Greenwald's life. These qualities shine through in *Kellie's Book* and invite the readers not only to share her experiences but also to dream and think about their own lives, and of all the possibilities and opportunities for learning and loving that are available for their own exploration.

Kellie loved telling me about herself. We decided that Kellie's stories held information that would provide a joyful guide for people with developmental challenges, their families, extended families, providers, and educators. People of all ages and walks of life can benefit from reading of Kellie's ability to meet her challenges. Kellie was proud that her father, Hank Greenwald, had published his memoirs. Could she do it, too? We envisioned an artistic, readable, professional approach to a book of publication quality. We discussed these goals each time we worked together, keeping Kellie's creative determination always geared toward her accomplishments. Kellie's innate sense of colorful composition is beautifully engaging, illustrating each idea of her story to open many emotional, as well as educational, doors for the reader.

Enjoy *Kellie's Book,* for that is our first goal. As Kellie's teacher, I assure you that we bring it to you straight from the heart.

Susan Vickery
Teacher
Victory Center for Arts and Communications
The Cedars of Marin

## A Note from a Proud Family

Kellie Greenwald's interest in art began at an early age with coloring books. Unfortunately, several of the books she was coloring belonged to her father. Her parents were quick to recognize her talent even though the 1979 San Francisco Giants didn't exactly wear green uniforms.

Kellie's mom, Carla, encouraged her development by enrolling her in various after-school arts programs, which included dramatics, painting and ceramics. Her work in ceramics has been widely acclaimed by critics, most notably her mother and father. Several of her pieces are on display at various locations throughout Northern California such as the Greenwalds' kitchen, living room and family room.

As an illustrator, Kellie leans toward the Impressionistic school, though as an infant her first spoken word suggested she favored the Dadaists. Her work in this book was done with Prismacolor Art Stix, which combine texture with richly pigmented color.

Over the years Kellie has shown that a person born with Down syndrome has as much to teach as she has to learn. She has opened the eyes of a great many people with respect to personality, capability and potential. As parents who once wondered if she would ever talk, concerns now focus on the admonition: "Don't let her near a microphone."

With the publication of this book it appears Kellie has now settled on a career. For the time being, at least, she has put aside such other pursuits as singing, poetry, day care center work, restaurant hostess and play-by-play broadcasting.

We trust this book will be not only a reflection of her artwork, but one whose words illustrate some of the innermost feelings we all share.

For my Parents, Carla And Hank,

AnD My brother, Doug.

In Memory of My Grandma, Mary Louise.

With love

Hi. My name is KELLIE. This is MY LiFe STORY. I WROTE This BOOK AND MADE ALL OF THE DRAWINGS.

I VVAS Born in SAN FRANCISco. WHen my MOTHER had me I had Down syndrome. When I WAS A BABY, About One Year old, I had open HEARt Surgery. now I have A pACemaker.

I hAve Two PARents And one BroTheR, They
ARe very speciaL To Me. I Love My whole
FAmiLy very much. They mean alot to me And
I Am impoRTant To Them.

When I was A little girl I Went to A School
Called Living And Learning Center. Even Though
it WAs hard for me  I tried My veRy Best. I had
A Speech Therapist  Who TAught me how To do
Sign language. My Teachers TAught me how to
Read and write.

When I was About Four years old   I WAs on a
Carousel ride. I had   aL ot of Fun When I was
in Disney WorLD I Like to pray. I like to Learn.

I enjoyed going To The high school Prom with
my friend HAYDEN. I feel pretty in my new dress
And My Flowers.

I Like music Because I love To sing. I Love
singing romantic music SOFTLY. I love to sing
LoudLy TOO. I like PlAYing my guitar when I
sing.

Exercise is very important. I like playing baseball at the college of Marin. I like playing with my friends.

I really enjoy being in the pool. I like to swim. Wearing a bikini is FUN.

I love my cat, Sweet Pea, I enjoy PLAYing with her, and TAKing care of her.

It is nice when I go on vacations. I enjoy sun and going to good restaurants. Going places and seeing new things is cool.

I like Being with my Friends At my Group home. I Like Being independent. I like To work on my skills. I hAVE MY own room with MY own computer. Cooking For everyone is Delicious And interesting.

I Like hAving MY Teachers around me When I am aT MY DaY Program. MY TeAchers Show me many opportuniTies. I love being an artist and Author.

ON MAY 26, 2000 I graduated from college of MAriN. I graduated with my friends. One of the teachers gave me A diPLoMA. They shook my hand.

Sometimes When I am sad I Feel Lonely. I missed My Friends After I graduated From college.

Sometimes I feel sad because I am confused, frustrated, and overwhelmed.

I Used To Work At Roush's Drug Store. I helped with customer services. I would TAKe Them to The Aisles to get products From A To Z.

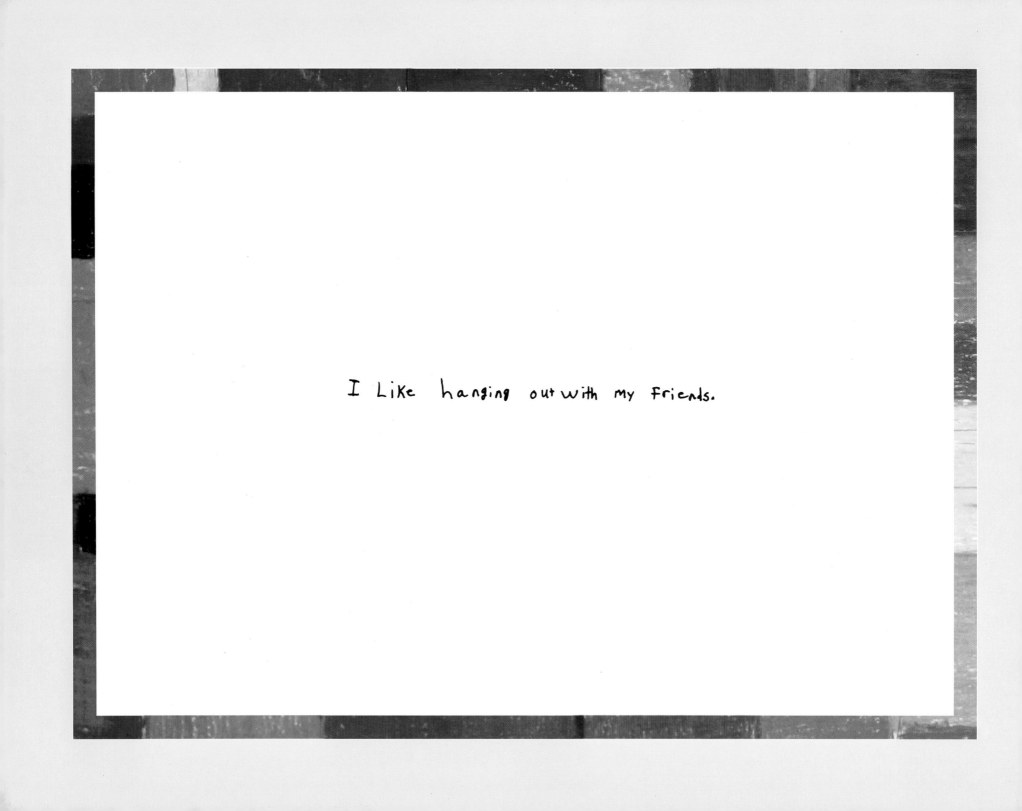

I Like hanging out with my friends.

I Am very happy That I have my own room. I
Am Looking Forward to getting A PLAce OF My
own someday in the future. I am happy That
I am Learning new Things. I am 29 Years old. I
have A boy Friend Who is the Same Age as
me. I am happy That I have my Family
in my Life.

Love is A Good Feeling. our Hearts Will be The SAme. My HEArt is sensitive And soft, Filled with Love. Sharing our hearts creates love and mAkes Love.

"My Grandma Mary Louise Reiter. I miss her."

"Do you think I look good in blue?"

"Oh, say can you see..."

"Another backhand winner."

"At my first prom. Hayden Roberts and I are taking it one step at a time."

"When I was a kid I was in Fiji and got to jam with the guys."

*"Mike Krukow just told me how he beat Walter Johnson, or was it Randy Johnson?"*

*"Jon Miller and Lee Jones like my impersonation of Jon doing Vin Scully."*

*"Actually, Ted, I'd have bunted in that situation."*

*"Thom Brennaman — my first love."*

*"Kuiper, I've got your number!"*

*"Okay Dodger fans, take this!"*

*"I told Dusty Baker not to sign for less than five years."*

"My brother needs a haircut."

"I sure love my family."

"My brother will be embarrassed when he sees this picture."

"On a visit to Boston we played in the park."

"She's the best mother I ever had."

"I want to broadcast someday with my brother."

*"Don't blame me. I don't pick out his ties."*

*"The Willie Mays-Kellie Greenwald statue."*

**"I DID IT!"**

*"We'll be back after this word from our sponsor."*

*"I only need one more homer to pass Barry."*

## Order Form

A portion of the proceeds from the sale of *Kellie's Book* will be donated to The Victory Center for Arts and Communications, a day program of The Cedars of Marin in San Anselmo, California. It was there that Kellie Greenwald wrote and illustrated this book with the guidance and encouragement of her teacher Susan Vickery.

For more information on the day program, contact The Victory Center for Arts and Communications at (415) 526-1350; or visit The Cedars of Marin website, www.thecedarsofmarin.org.

To order copies of *Kellie's Book*, photocopy the order form below and mail it, along with your check or money order, to the publisher; or to use a credit card, call Rayve Productions at our toll-free number, fax the order form, or order at our website, www.rayveproductions.com.

Price:        $24.95
Shipping:  $6.00 Priority Mail, for the first book + $2 each additional
Sales Tax:  California residents only, please add *7.75%* sales tax

***Rayve Productions*** 800-852-4890; fax 707-838-2220   Box 726, Windsor, CA 95492

### THE CEDARS OF MARIN

*Please photocopy form for orders by mail or fax.*

Name _____   Date _____

Address _____   Phone _____

City _____ State _____ Zip _____   Email _____

❏ Check Enclosed $ _____

❏ Charge my Visa/MC/Discover/AMEX $ _____        *Thank you!*

Credit card # _____ Exp. _____

Signature _____